Saskia Hühn

The Australian Connection

Paul Stewart

Cornelsen

The Australian Connection
Paul Stewart

Verlagsredaktion
Susanne Döpper

Umschlaggestaltung
Heike Börner, dia

Titelbilder
STOCK IMAGE/PIXLAND/ALAMY
Corel Library

Illustration
Annette Krause

Technische Umsetzung
Gisela Hoffmann

www.cornelsen.de

1. Auflage, 20. Druck 2009 / 06

Alle Drucke dieser Auflage sind inhaltlich unverändert
und können im Unterricht nebeneinander verwendet werden.

Druck: CS-Druck CornelsenStürtz, Berlin

ISBN 978-3-464-06807-6

Inhalt gedruckt auf säurefreiem Papier aus nachhaltiger Forstwirtschaft.

Contents

Chapter One

The trip of a lifetime

Alex sat on his bed and played the guitar quietly. The letter, in its official brown envelope, lay on his desk unopened. Alex looked at it, but made no move towards it.

He had been waiting for his exam results for eight long weeks. Now that they had finally arrived, he was too nervous to look at them. If he had passed, then everything was going to be fantastic. He would not only be able to go to university, but he would also be able to travel. That was all part of the deal. His mum had promised him that if he studied hard and got good grades, she would buy him a return air-ticket to anywhere in the world he wanted to go.

Alex looked across at the photograph on his bedside table. It was a black and white picture of a man and a boy. They were both sitting on the grass next to a pond, and grinning into the camera. A toy yacht lay on the boy's knees.

Alex sighed. He had been two-and-a-half, and his father had left home soon after. He hadn't seen him since then. Now – sixteen years later – he had the chance to meet him once again. So long as he had passed!

"Come on," Alex said to himself angrily. "What are you waiting for?"

And with that, he laid the guitar on the bed, got up and walked over to the letter. His fingers were shaking, as he opened the envelope. The next moment he screamed out with delight.

"YEAH!!!"

"Oh, that's wonderful news!" his mum exclaimed. "Well done, Alex! It's so good to know that you won't make the same mistake that I made."

When Alison had married Tom, she had thrown away the chance of going to university. It was a decision she had regretted since then.

"Now you can keep studying," she said, "and get some real qualifications."

Alex smiled, uncertainly. "But next year, yes?" he said.

Alison Reid smiled back. "It's all right," she said. "I haven't forgotten our deal. Have you thought about where you'd like to go?"

Alex looked down. Now that the moment had come, he felt embarrassed.

"Well?" she said.

"Australia," came the answer.

"Australia," his mum repeated.

Alex nodded.

"You want to go and visit your father?" she said.

"Do you mind?" he asked and expected the worst.

But his mum shook her head. "No," she said. "I don't mind. I always knew that one day you'd want to go. It's only natural. In fact, it's a pity Tom has been so bad at staying in contact."

Hearing her criticism made Alex feel strangely defensive towards the father he had grown up without.

"He's probably very busy," he said.

"Probably," his mum said quietly. "Anyway, I think the best thing now is for you to write him a letter. Tell him what's …"

Alex grinned. "I already have," he said.

Although short, the letter had taken him ages to write. To start with, he hadn't been sure whether to write *Dear Tom* or *Dear Dad*. After a lot of thought, he chose *dad* – after all, he *was* his father.

What was more, he knew that writing before he had received his exam results might be stupid. Despite the danger of being disappointed however, the week before – feeling both optimistic and excited – Alex *had* written.

Up in his room again, Alex wrote his address on the airmail envelope and read the letter through, especially the most important part.

I'll arrive in the second week of January, and plan to travel around Australia for six months – as long as my visa allows. I'd really like to see you.

It was all right, but was it clear enough what he wanted? Alex thought not, and added an extra sentence.

Would it be possible for me to come and stay for a little while?

"That's better," he said.

Satisfied at last, Alex put the letter into the envelope and took it down to the post-box on the corner. "Please write back soon," he said quietly, as the letter disappeared from view.

The next few months seemed never-ending. Although his mum was paying for the air-fare, it was up to Alex to earn his spending money, and so he had found work in a local factory.

KayCee Ltd. made kitchen cleaners, and it was Alex's job to fill, label and box the various soaps, bleaches and disinfectants they produced. The people he worked with were nice enough, but the job itself was unbelievably boring. Every day, he had to remind himself that it was only temporary; that by Christmas he would have saved enough to travel round Australia for six months.

The weeks passed, but no word came from Tom. Every morning Alex raced downstairs to check the post; every morning he was disappointed.

"I'm sure he *will* write," his mum said. "He was never very good at letters," she reminded him.

"I know," said Alex sadly.

As Christmas came nearer, Alex's sadness changed to

worry. Perhaps the letter had got lost in the post. Perhaps the Connells had moved. Or worst of all, perhaps Tom had decided that he didn't want to see his son at all.

Then, on 20th December – two days before he was due to stop working at the factory – the letter finally arrived. Alex was brushing his teeth when he heard the postman pushing the post through the letter-box. He hurried to the top of the stairs and looked down.

Lying by the door were several Christmas cards, and in among the white envelopes was a triangle of blue. There was no question. It was the corner of an airmail envelope.

This time Alex didn't hesitate. He raced downstairs, grabbed the letter and opened it.

Dear Alex,

Sorry I haven't written sooner, but I've been up to my eyes with work. It was great to hear from you, and we're all really looking forward to seeing you – I don't know what your plans are, but we've got a spare room and you're welcome to stay as long as you like.

By the way, congratulations on doing so well in your exams. Of course, I always knew you were clever. You drew the picture I'm enclosing when you were two years and nine months old, and there aren't many children that young who can write!

Let me know when you are arriving in Sydney, and I'll pick you up at the airport.

All for now. *Love, Tom*

Alex laid the letter down next to the telephone, and slowly opened the piece of paper which Tom had sent with the letter. It was a photocopy of a child's drawing.

There were three smiling people – all face and no body. The arms and legs were joined to the heads. Under the first person was the word *mummy*. Under the second, smaller person, *Alex*. And under the third, *daddy*.

As Alex stared at the picture he could almost remember drawing it. Suddenly his head was filled with other thoughts too, as if the picture had opened a door to the past. He remembered the orange and red ball they'd kicked around the park, he remembered sitting on his dad's lap as they went down the water-chute at the swimming-pool, he heard his dad as he explained that wasps sting but flies don't. And, for the first time, his dad was something more than the man grinning out of the photograph.

This was his real dad. The dad he was going to see in less than a month's time.

There were tears in his eyes as Alex folded up the picture and put it back into the envelope.

Chapter two

Hello Australia

As Alex queued to have his passport checked, he felt more and more confused. Half of him was excited about meeting his real father, half of him felt guilty about leaving his family behind.

He looked at his passport photo. It made him look younger than his eighteen years and the name next to it suddenly looked just as strange. Alexander Patrick Reid. His mum had changed his name from Connell when she'd married again, but Alex had already decided to change it back – as long as Tom didn't mind.

He looked round. His mum and Peter, Lucy and Danny, were still standing at the barrier. They waved happily at him.

"Have a wonderful time," Peter called.

Alex smiled as he tried to fight back the tears. He knew he was being ungrateful. Peter couldn't have been a better father to him – yet the fact remained that Tom Connell, not Peter Reid, was his real father. And as Alex finally walked through into the departure lounge, all he could think about was their coming reunion.

Thirty-eight hours later – after stops in Athens and Singapore – the plane landed at Sydney airport at 7.42, Tuesday, 8th January.

"Alex! Alex!" he heard as he left customs.

When he looked round, he noticed a tall woman with two small children. All three were waving at him: but why were there only three of them? Alex wondered. Where was Tom?

"I knew it was you," the woman said. "You haven't changed a bit!" she laughed and showed him the photo of the smiling toddler. "I'm Mary," she said. "Tom's wife. And these are our two kids, Dominic and Luke."

"Hello," said Alex. "They're ... younger than I thought they'd be," he added to Mary.

"Yeah, six and three," she said. "Tom took a long time to settle down when he got back to Australia," she added.

Alex nodded. "Where *is* Tom?" he asked.

"He'll be back in a couple of days," said Mary. "He had to go to London on business, I'm afraid. He was ..." Mary stopped as she suddenly realized what she had said.

"London?" Alex repeated. "Does he often go to London?"

Mary looked away. "Oh, now and then," she said vaguely. "And the trips are always so hectic."

But Alex was not interested in her excuses. Tom had not only never written, but he'd been to London – maybe hundreds of times – and not once got in contact. What kind of a man was his dad anyway?

By the time Alex had showered, changed into cooler clothes and had some breakfast, he was feeling less angry. Tom was in London. So what? Alex was going to have a fantastic time in Australia with or without Tom Connell.

"Now, are you sure you wouldn't like to have a sleep?" Mary asked for the tenth time.

Alex shook his head. "I'm too excited," he said.

"What about going swimming, then?" she asked.

"That would be great!" Alex grinned.

Half an hour later, they were all on Bondi Beach and put down blankets and towels on the hot, white sand. Mary had packed a huge picnic lunch, but Alex was neither hungry nor thirsty. All he wanted to do was get into that deep blue water, gently splashing on the sand.

"Be careful of the rip!" Mary called out, as he ran down to the water's edge.

Alex stopped. "What's that?" he asked nervously. "A kind of shark?"

From the way Dominic and Luke started laughing, Alex

knew at once that whatever else "a rip" might be, it was certainly not a shark.

"It's the Aussie word for current," Mary explained. "It can take you right out to sea if you're not careful."

"I *will* be careful," Alex promised.

"I'll go with him, mum," said Dominic and raced down the beach.

Alex smiled at the thought that a six-year-old would be able to rescue him. But as he watched the boy while he was darting around like a fish, his smile disappeared. The small kid was as much at home in the water as he was on land.

"Come on," Dominic shouted, as he swam out towards the breakers. "I'll show you how to body surf."

"That was brilliant," Alex said over tea, later that afternoon.

"You've certainly caught the sun," said Mary. "If you like, we could go down to one of the beaches south of Sydney tomorrow. Bateman's Bay is nice."

Before Alex could answer, the back door opened and a girl walked in. She was tall, about his age and – Alex thought – incredibly beautiful.

"Hi!" she said.

"Hello, Dani," Mary said. "Would you like something to drink? This is Alex."

"Yes, I guessed," she said as she looked him up and down. "I've heard all about you," she smiled.

"All good, I hope," said Alex shyly.

She grinned. "But not quite up to date," she said.

"Dani lives next door," Mary explained. "I don't know what I'd do without her. She's the babysitter for our two little monsters."

Dani smiled and turned back to Alex. "So," she said. "Tell me a little bit about yourself."

And Alex did. He explained about Tom and his mum, and

how he'd wanted to meet his real dad. And about the air ticket to anywhere in the world if he passed his exams ...

"Good-looking *and* clever!" Dani laughed.

Alex turned red. "What do you do?" he said.

"Now you're asking!" Mary said. "Dani's famous. Our local pop star!"

It was Dani's turn to blush.

"You're in a pop group?" said Alex. He tried not to sound too impressed. "What are they called?"

"*The Beat Crew,*" said Dani. "You won't have heard of us in England yet. But you will!" she added.

"You're good then, are you?" Alex said.

"We're on tonight at Coogee Bay," she said. "Why don't you come and see for yourself?"

Alex smiled. "Okay," he said.

"So, what did you think?" Dani shouted above the sound of the disco music which had replaced the band.

"You were good," he shouted back. "Very good." Alex had known she would ask that question and it was nice not to have to lie. *The Beat Crew* really were good. Two guitars, saxophone, drums and keyboards – Dani was on the keyboards.

"No criticisms at all?" she asked.

"Well," Alex said. "The bass guitarist's not much good, is he? I could do better than that!"

Dani shook her head. "Awful, wasn't he? He was just standing in for the night. Our bassist left for Japan last week and we haven't been able to replace him yet. I ..." Dani went quiet as she realized what Alex had just said.

"You play the guitar?" she said slowly.

Alex nodded.

"Do you play well?"

"Not bad," he said modestly.

Dani breathed in and looked at him. "Right," she said. "I'll pick you up at one o'clock tomorrow and take you to meet the others. If you can play, we could try you out tomorrow night." She suddenly stopped. "I'm going too fast," said Dani. "Sorry. I'll start again. Would Alex Reid ..."

"Connell," said Alex.

"Would Alex *Connell* like to audition for a place in the up-and-coming pop sensation, *The Beat Crew*?"

"Oh, yes," Alex grinned. "He certainly would."

The following night, Alex let himself into the Connells' house quietly. It was past one o'clock, and Mary and the kids were already asleep. Alex made his way to his room, threw himself on the bed and lay staring at the ceiling.

"That was the best day of my life," he whispered happily. "I'll never forget it."

And to make sure he didn't, he picked up his diary and began writing.

11 January - 1.45

I've been in Australia for exactly 66 hours and 3 minutes. And what a time I've had!

Tom wasn't at the airport to meet me (he's in London!!), but Mary, Dominic and Luke have all made me feel really at home. Been body surfing on Bondi Beach. Played my first live concert - $ 40 to show for it! And met Dani.

Dani Klavans - the most beautiful girl in the world. Long dark hair. Blue eyes. Golden skin. Perfect! Thank heavens Tom came from Sydney!

CHAPTER THREE

The island and the mountain

The next morning, Mary woke Alex at 10 o'clock with a cup of coffee.

"Did you have a good night?" she said, as she opened the curtains.

Alex winced at the bright light. Yes, it had been a good night; a very good night – and he had the headache to prove it.

"Perfect," he said quietly. "It's a pity it was just for the one night."

"I *am* glad," said Mary. "Now, I had a phone call from Tom while you were out. I'm afraid he's been delayed and won't be back till the 17th."

Alex sighed with irritation.

"He wanted to tell you himself how sorry he was," Mary continued. "But you weren't ... Anyway, I've had an idea. I think you should use the opportunity to see a bit more of the country. My brother lives in Adelaide and he's got a son, Kevin, who is your age. If you'd like to go, you're welcome to stay with them. South Australia is beautiful."

A phone call later, it was all arranged. Alex would spend the following week in Adelaide.

It was the vastness of the country – so different from anywhere he'd been in Europe – which struck Alex as the coach drove through the Australian countryside. There were, of course, small towns along the route, but beyond and between them, there were no houses or people to be seen.

Alex closed his eyes and remembered the figures he'd read in his guide book. Australia was the size of mainland USA; half as large again as Europe – yet its population was only 19.5 million. And, with his head full of the wonderful empty landscape that no photograph could ever show, he fell asleep.

It was dark when they finally arrived in Adelaide. Alex picked up his travel bag and sleepily left the coach.

"You must be Alex," came a voice.

Alex looked round. "Kevin Williams?" he said.

The young man grinned and held his hand out. "Welcome to Adelaide, mate," he said, and shook Alex's hand warmly.

"How did you recognize me so easily?" Alex asked. "Do I look that English?"

"Yeah, I can always tell a pom!" Kevin laughed.

Alex looked down at his jacket, jeans and trainers. Did he really look so different? Kevin saw Alex's confused face and laughed all the louder.

"I'm just joking, mate," he said. "Aunt Mary told me you'd be carrying a green and yellow bag. Come on, the car's parked round the corner. Are you hungry?"

"Starving!" said Alex happily. He liked Kevin's sense of humour, and already knew that they were going to get along really well.

As he talked over dinner with the Williams family – mum, dad, Kevin and his three younger sisters – Alex once again felt completely at home. Australians were *so* friendly. And as the meal came to an end, Kevin laid a map on the table and began to explain to Alex all the things he'd planned for that week.

"I thought we'd take the tent over to Kangaroo Island first," he was saying.

"Oh, you'll love it," said Mr Williams. "The animals there aren't afraid of people. They'll eat from your hand."

"What, kangaroos?" said Alex excitedly.

"And koalas!" the three girls added excitedly.

"And emus," Mrs Williams said. "And the possums can be a bit of a nuisance!" she laughed.

Twenty-four hours later, Alex was finding out for himself just what she had meant. All evening their camp-fire was surrounded by the cat-like animals looking for any unguarded food. And as they lay in their sleeping bags that evening, Alex and Kevin could hear the possums outside the tent that were trying in vain to break into their metal food-box.

"So what do you think of Kangaroo Island?" Kevin asked.

"It's wonderful!" said Alex. "In fact, I was just about to write to my family back in England to tell them exactly how wonderful it is. Do you mind if I put the torch on?"

"No, I can sleep through anything. See you in the morning."

"Goodnight," said Alex. He sat up, pulled his pen and a postcard from his bag and began writing.

> *Sunday*
>
> *Dear all,*
>
> *I'm having a fantastic time, although I haven't seen Tom yet – I'll explain in a letter.*
>
> *I've been body surfing on Bondi Beach, played live in a band, and am now on Kangaroo Island, south of Adelaide.*
>
> *It was cut off from the mainland thousands of years ago and the animals never learnt to be frightened of man. I fed biscuits to a wild kangaroo by hand, and stroked a koala! Lucy and Danny, you would love it here!*
>
> *Love, Alex*
>
> *Mr & Mrs Reid*
> *16 Meadcross Road*
> *Hedley*
> *Bucks.*
> *RN2 7BL*
> *England*

The picture on the front of the postcard was of Seal Bay; a wide, sandy beach covered with seals. Shortly after breakfast the following day, Alex was standing among them and took photographs of the huge, fearless animals.

The four days on Kangaroo Island raced by. Kevin took Alex to see the underground caves, to lie in the sun next to a blue lagoon and to snorkel around sunken shipwrecks. But better than all of these were their camp-fire conversations. As they sat and watched the sun set, Alex would ask question after question about his father.

"He was a fantastic uncle when I was a kid," Kevin laughed. "I don't see so much of him these days."

"Why?" Alex asked.

"I'm not sure," said Kevin, "In many ways, Tom's just a big kid himself. I think I got too old for him."

Alex nodded thoughtfully. From Alison's and Mary's, and now Kevin's descriptions, he was slowly beginning to get a picture of his father.

"He sounds very different from me," Alex said at last, and wondered again how they would get along when the two of them finally met.

On the Thursday morning, they returned the hired car and took the early ferry back to the mainland. Then, after a short stop in Adelaide – where they picked up clean clothes and Mr Williams' four-wheel drive – they left for Wilpena Pound, a natural amphitheatre in the Flinders Ranges.

As they drove north, the land became drier and drier. It was Alex's first experience of the world famous "Outback". They passed through ghost-towns which had been abandoned when the rains had failed. Except for a quick lunch next to some caves, decorated with Aboriginal paintings, they drove all the way without a break. Even so, it was dark when they arrived at the campsite. It wasn't until the following morning, when Alex left the tent, that he was able to look around.

"Wilpena" itself is an Aboriginal word which means *bent fingers,* Alex remembered. And that was just what the mountains looked like; a huge, cupped hand.

"That's the highest point, over there," Kevin said. "St Mary's Peak. It's 1190 metres high – not quite the Alps, but it's a difficult walk up. It'll take at least three hours, so we ought to leave soon. Before the sun gets too high."

"Okay," said Alex. "Why don't we miss breakfast and eat something as we go?"

"Good idea," Kevin agreed. "I'll fill the water bottles and we'll go."

It actually took over four hours to climb the mountain. There was no wind, there were no clouds, and the sun grew hotter and hotter as the time passed. The track was rocky and narrow – often it disappeared completely. And when Kevin and Alex finally reached the top, they were tired, hot and very sweaty.

"My shirt's wet through," said Kevin.

"Yeah, but look at the view," said Alex. "It's like standing at the top of a crater on the moon."

"Fantastic, isn't it?" said Kevin. "I remember we all came here once with Uncle Tom. *He* thought it looked like the moon too. I must have been about nine at the time. We sat here – just where we're sitting now – and he said something I'll never forget. He told me that he'd always wanted to be an astronaut when he was my age. Then he added, 'And I'll let you into a little secret. I still do! They all want me to get married and settle down, but I don't think I'll ever feel old enough to do that.' Funny, eh?" said Kevin.

Alex remained silent.

"Still, he settled down in the end," said Kevin. "Mary and …"

"He already had," Alex interrupted. "He'd already been married and … and ." Tears filled his eyes, his throat ached. "And he had me!" he shouted. "Me. His son!"

Embarrassed, Kevin changed the topic. "Look at the sky," he said.

Alex turned round. "It's just mist, isn't it?" he said. "It should make it a bit cooler."

Kevin shook his head. "Rain," he said. "All the way from England! Come on, let's go."

It was indeed rain, and when it hit – five minutes later –

Alex found himself in the heaviest downpour he had ever known. Within seconds, both Alex and Kevin were soaked to the skin, as they stumbled down the mountainside.

By the time they arrived back at the tent, the rain had stopped and their clothes were steaming in the hot sun.

"Your jacket's on fire," Alex laughed, and threw the water left in his bottle all over Kevin.

"Yeah?" Kevin grinned, as he picked up a bottle of suntan oil. "This is war!"

Alex was already half asleep as he climbed into his sleeping bag that night. His whole body felt tired and heavy. After they'd cleaned up the mess, Alex and Kevin had a shower, put on new clothes and ate in the Wilpena Pound Restaurant. For Alex, it had been – despite, or perhaps because of the rain – another perfect day, spoilt only by Kevin's stories of Tom Connell.

Alex had been angry. That Tom had not kept in contact was one thing, but to pretend that his own son did not exist was quite another. He remembered that Tom was expected back home that evening and was glad he wouldn't be there to meet him.

Let him see how *he* likes it, he thought, as he went to sleep.

Twice, Alex put off his return to Sydney. The first time, to go out fishing on Mr Williams' boat; the second, to spend the day winetasting in the Barossa Valley. He was so annoyed with his father that he didn't care when – or even if – he saw him. In fact, if it wasn't for a certain dark-haired, blue-eyed girl, Alex might have remained in Adelaide for the rest of his stay.

As it was, on 23 January, at quarter past eight in the evening, Alex waved goodbye to the Williams family for the last time as the coach left for Sydney. In his diary, he wrote:

Wednesday, 23 January

I'm returning to Sydney with very mixed feelings!

Chapter Four

The big decision

"Alex!" said Mary, as she opened the door. "You're back. Did you have a good time?"

"Fantastic!" said Alex.

"I knew you would," said Mary. "Come into the kitchen. There's someone to see you."

Alex felt nervous. Fifteen years, he'd waited for this moment. Fifteen years! Suddenly, all he had to do was go through the kitchen door to be reunited with his father.

"Come on, then," said Mary.

"I'll be with you in a minute," said Alex. "I'm just hanging my jacket up."

Now that the time had finally arrived, Alex wanted to run and hide. But he couldn't turn back now. He placed his hand on the door handle, took a deep breath, and pushed the door open.

"Dani!" he exclaimed, as he saw who the person really was.

"So, the wanderer returns," Dani said.

"I nearly didn't," Alex grinned. He turned to Mary. "Where's Tom? Has he been delayed again?"

Mary sighed. "Oh, Alex," she said. "He got home last Thursday, but he had to go away again. Singapore, this time. He won't be back until Friday."

"Friday," Alex repeated. "That's the day after tomorrow."

"Never mind," he smiled bravely.

"The thing is," Dani said, "you might not want to be here on Friday."

"Why's that?" Alex asked.

And Dani told him. She explained that everyone in the band thought he played really well, that they knew he was only in Australia for six months, but that if he'd like to play with them until then, he was welcome. Maybe after that, she suggested, he could extend his visa. It was a big decision, Alex realized. It would mean he'd miss Tom again. It would mean he wouldn't get to see so much of the country. But then again …

"When do I start?" he grinned.

"Two hours ago!" Dani said. "We've got a week of gigs in Melbourne which start tonight. But we've got to leave now if we're going to get there on time."

Alex looked at Mary.

"You go ahead," she said. "I'll explain to Tom."

With its tall, grey Victorian buildings, Melbourne reminded Alex a lot of London. What was more, it was raining!

"Home from home, eh?" said Pete the drummer, nodding at the wet streets.

"It doesn't always rain in London," Alex said. He was beginning to get a bit fed up with all the jokes about English weather. "25 inches a year we get. That's less than Sydney, Melbourne, Brisbane …"

"Yeah, but it's every day," Pete said. "When I was there, it was drizzle, drizzle, drizzle – every morning, the sky was the colour of wet cement."

Alex laughed.

At that moment, Dani, who was map-reading, suddenly shouted out. "Pitcairn Avenue! It's down there on the right."

The wheels screeched as Terry raced round the corner, and stopped outside a club called Angelo's. They all looked out of the windows of the mini-bus. It was certainly the right place. Along the front wall there were several posters which were advertising the evening show.

Below the words, was a photo of the band. Terry, Pete, Joe and Dani, together with the old bass guitarist.

"We'll have a new poster done," Dani said to Alex. "I promise. As soon as we get back to Sydney."

Alex nodded. "I'd like that," he said.

Yes, if Alex was in the band, he wanted people to know it. That first concert in Sydney had shown him how much he liked being on stage. The dancing audience, the applause, the shouts for "More!" – he loved it all. Everyone who plays in a band dreams of becoming rich and famous. Alex himself didn't mind so much about the money, but his taste of fame had made him want more!

The Beat Crew had a hectic schedule in Melbourne. Most nights they played two gigs; at colleges, clubs and discos. The high point of the trip for Alex however, was an appearance on television. *It's Saturday Night!* was watched by millions of young people all over Australia and, with this in mind, Alex grinned happily into the camera as he sang and played.

"So, you want to be famous, do you?" Dani asked him, as she put suntan oil on his shoulders.

Alex rolled over and looked up. "Who doesn't?" he said.

It was Sunday, and Alex and Dani had taken the opportunity of their only free afternoon, to spend some time at the sea. They had borrowed the mini-bus and driven round the coast to Phillip Island. The beaches there were long and empty and, as the sun travelled slowly across the sky, the pair of them spent the day swimming, lying in the sun and getting to know one another better.

"I love it all," he said. "The hotel rooms, writing songs, playing live ..."

"Being in the spotlight!" Dani laughed.

Alex went red, as he wondered what Dani must think of him. "It's all so new," he explained.

She looked at him silently. Then she said, "You're different from Australian men. Not so macho!"

"Is that bad?" Alex asked.

"No," Dani smiled, and without another word, she bent down and kissed him.

As their mouths touched, Alex felt he was melting. He put his arms around her body and held her close to him. If playing in the band was the cake, then his feelings for Dani were the cherry on the top. And as everything was going so perfectly, he suddenly no longer cared that he had still not met his father. In fact, he didn't care if he never saw Tom at all!

This is what's important, Alex realized, as he touched Dani's skin.

Alex woke up a couple of hours later and looked round. He shivered. It was getting dark and a cold wind was blowing in from the sea. Dani lay beside him.

"Come on," said Alex, gently shaking her.

Dani opened her eyes. "What time is it?" she asked.

"Half five," said Alex.

"Good," she said. "We're not on stage until midnight, so we've got plenty of time. There's one more thing I want to show you."

They packed up and went through the dunes to a beach on the other side of the island. In contrast to the empty one where they had spent the day, Summerland Beach was full of tourists. Hundreds of people were standing on a wooden platform and looking down at the floodlit beach below them.

"What are they doing?" Alex asked.

"Watching *those,*" she said, and pointed to a small bird waddling up the beach.

"It's a penguin!" he exclaimed.

"*Eudyptula minor,* to be exact," said Dani. "The Little Blue Penguin. They build nests in holes they dig in the sand-dunes, and every evening at this time, they return from the sea with a huge fish-supper for their babies. Sweet, eh?"

But Alex didn't think it was sweet. Under the lights, the little penguins looked lost and afraid. It seemed wrong to him that the birds' daily fishing trip had become a piece of theatre. On the other hand, he didn't want to upset Dani.

"I wonder if *they* enjoy it," he said quietly.

Dani looked at him. "I thought you liked being in the spotlight," she said.

"*I'm* not a penguin," said Alex.

It was their first disagreement and, although not serious, it spoiled the atmosphere. As they drove back to the hotel, they neither talked nor looked at each other. It was only when they reached the car-park that they spoke – and then it was at the same time.

"Look, I'm ..."

"I had a ..."

They both stopped, looked at one another and laughed. Dani reached over and took his hand.

"I didn't know it would upset you," she said.

"I thought you were criticizing my dreams. The fame, and that," said Alex, looking away.

"Idiot," she said softly. "I wouldn't do that."

Alex turned. "I'm sor..." His apology, however, was cut short by Dani's kiss.

"Listen," she said, as she pulled away. "We're free after tonight. Why don't we go away somewhere together? Byron Bay is nice."

"That would be great," said Alex.

"It's a deal, then," she said and smiled. "Come on," she added, a moment later. "We'd better go in now. The others will think we've got lost!"

As they walked into the hotel, the man at reception called over to Alex.

"There was a phone call for you. From a Mrs Mary Connell. She asked if you could ring back."

Alex nodded. "Thanks," he said.

He was sure that she was phoning to ask when he was coming back. Tom was probably going on another business trip. The question was, why hadn't Tom himself phoned?

"I'll do it later," he said to Dani. "Let's go and change."

It wasn't until the Wednesday morning that Alex finally called back. True, he'd been busy. The band had been booked for three gigs on the Monday, and they had spent all of Tuesday learning a new song. But that wasn't the only reason. Alex was still angry with his father, and if the man was now feeling bad, well, so much the better.

"Hello?" came a familiar voice.

"Hello Mary, it's Alex. Is Tom there?"

"You've just missed him," said Mary.

Alex laughed. The situation was getting ridiculous. "Have you got his work number?" he asked.

"He's visiting clients all day," Mary said, and laughed too. She could also see the funny side of it. "I can't believe it's taking you two so long to meet."

"Perhaps we never will," said Alex.

"Oh, don't say that," said Mary, serious again.

"Do you think he'd mind, then?" Alex asked.

"Mind!" said Mary. "He's being unbearable. Like a little kid waiting for Christmas – a Christmas that never arrives!"

Alex smiled to himself. Kevin had said that Tom had never really grown up.

"He hasn't got long to wait now," said Alex. "I'm back on Thursday. I'll try to come to the house in the afternoon, but if not, I'm playing at *Sabrina's Bar* in the evening. We could meet there."

"As long as you do," Mary laughed. "I can't put up with Tom's miserable face much longer."

Alex smiled to himself. "I promise," he said.

CHAPTER FIVE

The face in the crowd

The journey back to Sydney that Thursday was a nightmare. They left at nine, but four and a half hours later on they had only travelled forty miles. The problem was a puncture. Normally, it should have taken ten minutes to change the wheel, but when they opened the boot, they found that the spare tyre was also flat. And there was no foot pump. Terry, who was responsible for the car, walked back along the road to a garage they had passed earlier. It was only when he returned – two hours later – that he discovered the jack was broken.

"Oh, no!" he shouted, and threw the useless piece of metal to the side of the road.

"Now what?" Dani asked. "We've got to be on stage at seven."

"You don't need to tell me," said Terry. "I'll try to flag someone down."

He picked up the broken jack and waved it at the oncoming car. It didn't stop. Neither did the next car, or the next car, or the car after that. And as the time passed – five minutes, quarter of an hour, half an hour, an hour – Alex realized that Australians were no friendlier than anyone else. In the end, when a car did finally stop, the driver was Vietnamese.

Luckily, he was driving a four-wheel drive, and the jack was big enough to lift the mini-bus without any difficulty. Ten minutes later, they thanked the man and drove off again. But not for long. They hadn't got more than ten miles when there was a sudden thud, and the windscreen was splashed with blood.

"We've hit something!" Pete shouted.

"Well done!" Terry said, as he braked and jumped out.

It was clear at once what had happened. The cow – which

must have escaped from its field – had come too near to the road. When the mini-bus struck the side of its head, the force and weight of the overloaded vehicle had proved a fatal combination. The cow had died at once.

"Didn't you see it?" said Pete, looking down at the dead animal.

"What do *you* think?" Terry said angrily. "Did you? The sun's so bright, I can hardly see anything."

"Well, that makes me feel *really* good," said Dani.

"If you can do any better, *you* drive!" Terry shouted.

"Don't talk to her like that," Alex shouted back.

"What are you going to do about it?" Terry demanded, turning on Alex.

"Just calm down, all of you," Joe said, stepping between Terry and Alex. "We're all okay. The cow isn't, but *we* are. Right? Let's just go and do this gig in Sydney, then we can have a whole week off – a week when we don't have to see each other. Okay?"

The others remained silent.

"Okay?" Joe repeated.

"Okay," they said quietly.

It was as they were returning to the mini-bus that they heard the noise: the plaintive sound of a baby who had lost its mother. They turned round, and there it was, a small calf which was standing some yards away.

"Poor little thing," said Dani. "We can't just leave it."

"Well, we can't take it with us," said Joe. "We'll stop at the next telephone and report what we've seen. Seen, not *done*! We don't want to be delayed even longer. The police can contact the farmer."

And so, with Terry back in the driver's seat, they drove off once again and, after a short stop to allow Joe to phone the police – he didn't trust Dani not to tell them the truth – and report the calf they'd seen next to its dead mother, they drove on towards Sydney as fast as they could.

If everything had gone well from then on, they would have arrived at about four o'clock. Unfortunately, everything did *not* go well. By the middle of the afternoon they were driving through the Blue Mountains, about 30 miles from Sydney. Suddenly, the engine began to lose power and, as the mini-bus came to a halt, everyone looked at Terry again.

"Why are we stopping?" asked Pete.

"To look at the view," said Terry sarcastically. "I don't know why we're stopping. Something must be wrong with the engine."

And with that, he climbed out of the van, slammed the door and walked away; this time towards a hotel they had passed a couple of miles back.

Dani looked round at Alex, and smiled. "It seems as if we're not meant to play in Sydney tonight," she said.

Alex nodded. "But I've got to," he said. "I promised."

"Promised who?"

"It doesn't matter," said Alex. And then, when he saw Dani's surprised face, he added, "I'll tell you later."

Alex didn't feel like talking. It was cold outside, and everyone had stayed in the mini-van. He didn't want them all to know about his family situation. And so, with nothing better to do, Alex decided to bring his diary up to date.

He described the events of the past week in detail. The hotel, the concerts, the conversations, the new song, the afternoon on the beach with Dani, the phone call from Mary, his feelings about Tom. Everything.

Once we'd cleaned the blood off, the mini-bus looked fine – except for a small dent. Dani and I wanted to tell the police what had really happened, but Joe wouldn't let us. He said we'd get held up and miss the concert. In the end we had to agree, but we both felt very bad about it. Unfortunately, the accident must have caused some damage to the engine. At 3.46, we broke down in the middle of the Blue Mountains. It serves us right for lying to the police! Terry went to get help over an hour ago, but so far ...

"There he is," Dani suddenly shouted.

Alex looked up. A breakdown truck, with *Ron's Garage* written along the side, had stopped next to them. Terry and a tall man in an overall – Ron, himself – jumped out. Alex returned to his diary.

5.12. Help has arrived! If the damage isn't too serious, we should still make it to "Sabrina's" on time.

The good news was that the engine was *not* badly damaged. In fact, it took Ron less than a minute to reconnect the wire which had come loose, and when he turned the key, the mini-bus started as if nothing had ever been wrong. The bad news was that he wanted $ 200 for coming out.

Two hundred dollars! That was as much as they would earn between them for the gig at *Sabrina's*. The man was clearly a crook, but as he was holding the keys, there was nothing they could do but pay him.

The day had been awful, but the moment Alex stepped on stage, he forgot all about it. The sight of the excited faces all waiting to be entertained was the only thing that mattered.

"This is our latest song," Joe shouted. "Two ... Three ... Four ..." and they were off.

The band danced as they played. The audience danced with them. Some of them knew the song and were singing along.

Jumpy!
I'm feeling jumpy
When you come, when you go,
When you stop and say "hello"
You make me jumpy!

This is GREAT!!! Alex thought happily. He looked round at Dani and grinned.

"Yeah!" she screamed.

Song after song, they got better and better. The band, the audience; *everyone* was having a fantastic time. And then Alex saw the face.

It was near the end of their set, and they were playing the last song but one, called *Earthquake*. Alex had to play his bass guitar extra loud so that it really felt as if the earth was shaking. Suddenly, it was his fingers which were shaking instead. He played a wrong note.

"Pull yourself together!" he said angrily.

He closed his eyes and concentrated on the song. *You move me like an earthquake, earthquake.* But he couldn't forget the face; he could pretend it wasn't there. Slowly, Alex opened his eyes, and there it was. The face of Tom Connell, smiling back at him.

"Dad," Alex whispered to himself.

Chapter six

Into the rain forest

As the last song of the evening came to an end, the lights went out. While the crowd was cheering and clapping, Pete, Terry, Dani and Joe left by the side of the stage. Normally, Alex would have gone with them. But not tonight. Tonight, the backstage drink would have to wait.

When the lights came on again, the audience groaned. They all knew there would be no more live music that night. And, as Alex jumped down onto the dance-floor, a couple of girls asked him for "just one more song". Alex simply smiled and walked past them. In front of him, with a huge grin on his face, was Tom Connell.

"Hello ... Tom," Alex muttered, as he went to shake hands.

"We can do better than that," Tom said. He ignored Alex's hand and hugged him instead. "Hello, son," he said.

"Hello, dad," Alex whispered. His throat ached, and there were tears in his eyes.

"Come on," said Tom. "Let's have a drink."

Their conversation was awkward at first. Tom was obviously trying hard to make his son feel comfortable, but the more he laughed and joked, the more angry Alex became inside. Fifteen years, and not a word. Fifteen years! Finally, he could keep his feelings bottled up no longer.

"You didn't even send me a Christmas card!" he shouted. "I can understand that you might forget my birthday. But Christmas! Every year I hoped and prayed that you would remember. But no. Nothing! Can't you imagine how that made me feel?"

"Alex, I ..."

"You're my dad! I mean, Peter is great. He is everything a boy could want from a father. But he isn't *my* father. He's Lucy's and Danny's. Not mine. No, *my* father abandoned me when I was three years old. Why?" he cried. "Wasn't I good enough for you? Didn't you like me?"

Alex knew he was losing control, and the last thing he wanted to do was start crying. He finished his beer and banged the glass down angrily on the table.

"I'll get us another drink," said Tom quietly.

When he returned, Alex was staring down at the carpet.

"Alex," he said. "All I can say is, I'm sorry. I got it wrong. You had a new life, a new family. I didn't think you'd *want* to hear from me. I thought you'd hate me," he added.

Alex looked up. "Mum explained why you left," he said. "I didn't hate you because of that ... But to pretend I had never even been born ..." He stopped.

Alex realized that his anger had disappeared. In its place was a deep sadness. All those years he had wanted to meet his father and now he was shouting at him. He knew he had a choice. Either he could forgive Tom Connell, or he could walk away and never see him again.

He picked up his glass and took a mouthful of beer. "It's in July," he said.

Tom grinned. "The seventh," he said. "Did you *really* think I could ever forget the day you were born. Look, I can't undo what I've already done," he said. "But I'll make it up to you. I promise."

Alex nodded. *Nothing* could make up for his fatherless childhood.

"Tell you what," Tom continued. "I've got some time off. Why don't we take a trip up to Queensland? You'll love it there. Just you and me. What do you say?

Before Alex could say anything Dani appeared at the table.

"Hi!" he said.

Dani looked embarrassed. "It's okay," she said. "I know you two have got a lot to talk over. I just came to say I'll go now, so I'll see you later. I'm going to get everything packed," she added, and winked at Alex.

And before Alex could answer, she had turned and gone.

"What was that about?" said Tom.

"I forgot," said Alex. "We'd planned to go up to Byron Bay.

"Oh, it's beautiful there," said Tom. "If you ... I mean, I'd understand if ..."

But Alex had already made up his mind. "No," said Alex decisively. "You and I are going to Queensland."

They quickly emptied their glasses and took a taxi home. Alex, however, did not follow Tom into the house. Instead, he went next door and knocked softly at the door. Dani answered it.

"Hello," she said, surprised to see him. "I expected you two to talk all night."

Alex smiled. There would be time enough to talk on their trip to Queensland. He looked into Dani's eyes.

"I've got something to tell you," he said.

Dani laughed nervously. "Well, you'd better come in then!" she said.

Although she said that it didn't matter; there would be other trips; that *of course* he must go, Alex knew that Dani was deeply disappointed. And with her brave smile and sad eyes, she looked *so* beautiful.

Alex moved closer and put his arms round her. Dani pulled away and looked up at him.

"Let's go upstairs," she whispered.

Alex smiled. "I think I'm falling in love with you," he whispered.

"Only think!" said Dani, pretending to be angry.

"I *know* I am," he said.

And as she took his hand and led him into her room, Alex felt as if it was a dream come true.

"I didn't hear you come in last night," Tom said.

He and Alex were sitting in the four-wheel drive. They had been sitting there for the past six hours, most of it spent silently.

Alex was thinking about Dani. And when he noticed the turn-off to Byron Bay he suddenly felt like telling Tom to turn around and go back. But Tom had spoken first and, for a terrible moment, Alex thought that his dad must be able to read his mind.

He looked round. Tom was grinning.

"*Mary* didn't hear you either," he said.

"That's because I didn't come in!" said Alex.

"Oh, yeah?" said Tom, raising his eyebrows.

"We had a lot to talk about," Alex said.

Tom smiled. "No regrets, then?"

"Pardon?"

"About the trip," he said. "You wouldn't have preferred to stay with Dani?"

Alex swallowed. "We're only going away for a week," he said – to himself, as much as to Tom.

"Yeah. We'll be back before you know it," he said cheerfully. "We should come to the Queensland border soon."

"Is it far after that?" Alex asked.

To his surprise, Tom began to laugh and threw Alex the map. "Take a look," he said.

"Cape Tribulation, did you say?" said Alex, as he searched along the coastline.

"Yes," said Tom. "It's north of Cairns."

Finally, Alex found the name, and gasped. He didn't think he would ever get used to the size of the country.

"It's over a thousand miles from Sydney!" he exclaimed.

"And we're not even half way yet," said Tom. "I'd get some sleep if I were you."

But Alex could not sleep. There was too much to see. The Gold Coast with its casinos and bright lights; the farmland, green with ripe sugar cane, and countless one-street towns. They stopped for petrol, but that was all. Brisbane, Rockhampton, Mackay, Townsville; the place names flashed past them as they continued through the night.

It was only when he suddenly woke up that Alex realized he *had* fallen asleep after all. The tarmac road had come to an end, and the four-wheel drive was driving slowly along a muddy track through dense rain forest. It was getting light.

"Are we nearly there?" Alex asked sleepily.

Tom laughed. "That's what you always used to ask when you were a little kid," he said. "Every time we went for a long drive. Some things never change."

Alex looked away. He never found it easy to talk early in the morning.

"About two hours to go," Tom said. "As long as the road stays good."

"*Good!*" Alex exclaimed. "This is the worst road I've ever been on."

"In rainy weather, it all ends up under water," said Tom. "The last time I came up, I was stuck between flooded rivers for two days."

Alex continued to look out of the side window. It was the most exotic scenery he had ever seen. Thick mangrove swamps, rope-like lianas, tall trees with plants clinging to their sides – plants which Europeans only saw growing indoors in pots. Multi-coloured butterflies flew past the car. Giant lizards watched them from the shadows.

"Uh-oh," said Tom, as he suddenly braked.

Alex looked up. The reason they had stopped was clear at once. A river crossed the road just in front of them and, although it wasn't that wide, the water looked very rough.

"What do we do now?" he asked.

"See how deep it is," Tom answered simply, as he climbed out of the car.

Alex followed him to the water's edge. Muddy and brown, it looked like a river of chocolate. It was impossible to tell how deep it was.

"Are you sure it's safe?" said Alex.

"I'll try not to get washed away," Tom smiled.

"That wasn't what I meant," he said, and pointed at the red and white sign on a tree. DANGER – CROCODILES!

"They don't attack if you don't disturb them," said Tom, as he waded into the water.

Alex could only hope he was right.

Fortunately, Tom was *not* eaten by a crocodile. Even more fortunately, at its deepest, the water only came up to Tom's knees, and the four-wheel drive crossed the river with no problems. Two hours later, they arrived at a hostel, deep within the rain forest at the foot of Mount Sorrow.

The next couple of days went far too quickly for Alex. He and Tom went walking through the steaming rain forest; they followed the boardwalk through the mangrove swamp; they rode horses along the sandy beach; they visited a crocodile reserve. Alex found himself surrounded by birds and insects, trees and flowers that he had only ever seen before on television.

"It's fantastic!" Alex said, again and again, as he saw more and more wonderful sights. "Really fantastic!"

"I'm glad you like it," said Tom. "I love it here. The trouble is, it's all changing. People from the cities are buying up the land and building holiday homes. Slowly but surely, the forest is being destroyed."

Alex looked at Tom. The trip had been wonderful, so far. And yet it was not how Alex had imagined it would be. He felt somehow that he had lost a father, but found a friend.

After a final walk – to the top of Mount Sorrow – Tom and Alex packed up the four-wheel drive and left. By midday, they were back at the river which had been so full and fast before. Now, it was just a shallow stream and Tom drove across easily.

Alex turned and looked back through the rear-window at the rain forest. Beautiful and remote, it had remained untouched for thousands of years. Now, all that had changed, and if strict laws were not soon made, the rain forest and everything in it would disappear for ever.

"It's so sad," he said.

Tom nodded. "People can be very, very stupid," he agreed angrily.

As they left the rain forest behind and the roads improved, Tom began to cheer up. He told Alex all about *Gypsy Woman*, the boat he shared with his brother, which was moored in Cairns.

"I thought we'd take her out onto the reef," he said.

"The Great Barrier Reef," Alex said excitedly.

"That's the one," Tom smiled.

Alex grinned. He knew all about the Great Barrier Reef, of course. He'd learnt about it in geography lessons and had always wanted to see the multi-coloured coral for himself. Now he was going to do just that.

"Is it as wonderful as it looks on film?" he asked.

"Better," Tom answered. "A million times better."

Chapter seven

Father and son

After a night at the Reef Motel in Cairns, Tom and Alex were up early the next morning. The sun was just rising as Tom steered them out of the harbour.

Gypsy Woman was a sailing boat, 9 metres long and painted blue and white. Because there was no wind at all that morning, Tom had left the sails rolled up, and started the engine instead.

"How far are we going?" Alex asked.

"Just near Grafton Passage," said Tom. "The coral's good there. It should take us about an hour and a half."

As they left the buildings of Cairns far behind them and Alex looked round at the endless blue water, he suddenly felt very small.

"Makes you realize how insignificant we are, doesn't it?" said Tom.

Alex looked at him and smiled. It was curious how often they were thinking exactly the same thing.

"Right," said Tom. "If you'd like to take the tiller, I'll get us both some breakfast."

They had coffee with rolls that Tom had brought with him from the motel. Afterwards, as Alex lay back on the deck – warm and full – and stared up at the clear blue sky, he knew that he had never been happier.

"The snorkelling equipment is in the cupboard at the bottom of the stairs," Tom said. "Could you go and fetch it? We're not far now."

While Alex was down below, he heard the sound of the anchor grating on rock below the boat. With his arms full, he raced up on deck.

"Are we there?" he asked excitedly.

"We are!" said Tom.

Alex looked over the side. He saw fish swimming in and out of the stone fingers of multi-coloured coral.

"It looks even better under water," said Tom, as he changed into his trunks.

With their flippers, mask and snorkel in place, Tom and Alex sat on the side of the *Gypsy Woman*, and dropped backwards into the water.

From the moment he first looked around, Alex thought he was in paradise. Tom was right. In real life, the reef *was* a million times better than on television. At least!

Again and again, Alex took a deep breath and dived down. He saw orange fish, pink fish, red, yellow and blue fish. He saw fish with spots and fish with stripes. He saw shoals of thin, silver fish that darted this way and that, all together, like a curtain blowing in the wind. It was fantastic! It was hypnotic! And it was only when he heard Tom shouting that Alex finally looked up.

"You should come out now," he said. "The sun's too hot on the back of your head. You'll get sunstroke."

"What time is it?" Alex called back.

"Ten to twelve," said Tom.

Alex could hardly believe his ears. He had been in the water for nearly three hours, and it hadn't seemed more than five minutes!

After lunch, Alex read and lay in the sun and listened to his Walkman, and read a bit more ... He was bored! All he wanted to do was return to the underwater world he had discovered. And when, at last, the sun did begin to cool down, Alex was back in the water before Tom had finished saying that it would be okay now for another swim.

This time, Alex swam further away from the boat. He followed the coral round to the far side of the reef where it formed a cliff which disappeared down to the sea-bottom, fifty metres below him.

For a while, he watched small orange and white fish swimming in and out of the tentacles of a giant sea anemone. Then, when a blue fish tried to do the same, it was caught at once.

"Clever," Alex thought.

He swam a little further round. The sea was colder here. Alex shivered. Then, suddenly, to his left he saw a movement. And then again. He rose to the surface, looked round and saw the terrible sight of a black fin cutting through the water. It was a shark. A SHARK!

His body went stiff. All he could think was *I'm going to die.*

The next moment Alex was swimming frantically back to the boat. His arms and legs splashed wildly, his head went from side to side, his heart felt as if it was going to explode. He looked round. The fin was still there, and the *Gypsy Woman* seemed no nearer.

"Faster! Faster!" he said to himself.

And when he finally reached the side of the boat, he called up to Tom.

"QUICK! QUICK!" he shouted. "There's a SHARK!"

Why wasn't Tom helping him? Why was he standing there holding his stomach? So he had stomach-ache – he could deal with that later. "GET ME OUT!" Alex screamed.

And then he realized the reason for Tom's aching stomach. He was laughing. Laughing so much he was bent over in pain. He was bright red and tears were running down his cheeks.

"GET ME OUT!" Tom copied Alex's terrified cries. "If you could have seen yourself! Splash, splash, splash. Get me out!" he repeated, and started laughing again.

"It's just a *basker,* mate," he said when he was finally able to speak. "It can't hurt you. No teeth!" he added.

Alex nodded. He pulled himself out of the water and started drying himself with his towel. While he had been watching Tom laughing, he had remembered something from the past. They had been at a horse-jumping show. A horse had broken away from its owner, and run across the grass towards Alex. He had screamed in horror as the giant animal had got closer. And his dad – what had he done? Then – as now – he had laughed at his son's fear. And for his part, then – as now – Alex hated him for it.

"I *said* I was sorry," Tom said.

"And *I* said it doesn't matter," said Alex.

"If it doesn't matter, then stop sulking," said Tom.

"I'm not sulking," said Alex. Sulkily.

Alex looked out across the bay. The pair of them were sitting on Whitsunday Island, a tiny spot on the map, north of Mackay. It was sandy. It had palm trees. It was the desert island of Alex's dreams.

Tom *had* felt sorry for laughing at Alex and, to make it up to him, he had arranged the trip. He'd booked a yacht, the *Thekla,* to take them across from the mainland. And an hour earlier, he and Alex had been left with their tents and backpacks, and enough food and water to last for four days – which was when they would be picked up again.

"Just like Robinson Crusoe," Tom had said.

Although Alex was excited about the trip to the island, Tom was right – he *was* sulking.

"Come on," said Tom suddenly. "Let's go for a swim."

The water certainly looked inviting, but Alex didn't move.

"There are no sharks here," said Tom. "Not even baskers. I promise!"

Alex looked at him. The man was trying so hard!

"Okay," he said.

"Great," said Tom, and jumped to his feet. "Last one in the water cooks dinner," he shouted, as he raced off across the sand. Alex ran after him. His legs were younger, stronger. He overtook Tom just before the water's edge and splashed into the sea.

"I won!" he shouted.

"You won," said Tom, and dived down out of sight. The next moment, he grabbed Alex's legs and pulled him under the water.

"Are we friends again?" he asked, as they both came back to the surface.

Alex smiled. Kevin was right; Tom Connell *was* just like a kid. "Of course we are," he said.

Everything was so dry that it took no time to light the fire and, as the sun set, Tom and Alex sat on the beach and ate huge amounts of rice and vegetables. To Alex, food had never tasted so good.

The rain started just as they had finished their meal.

"Let's get inside the tent," said Tom. "It's probably just a shower, we'll leave the washing-up till tomorrow."

"This is a *shower*!" Alex said an hour later, as the torrential rain continued to beat against the side of the tent.

"At least we're dry in here," said Tom.

But he had spoken too soon. At that moment, Alex felt the first *drip, drip, drip* of the rain coming through the roof. Soon, the water was coming in at twenty different points. There was nothing they could do as everything slowly became wet – their sleeping bags, their towels, their clothes. *Everything!*

It was getting light by the time the rain finally stopped. Neither Alex nor Tom had been able to sleep. They left the tent and looked around. The clouds were disappearing, and as the sun rose, everything started to steam. It was only when they went to make some breakfast that they found that it would not only be impossible to make a fire, but the unusually high storm tides had washed away all their cooking utensils from the beach.

"See," Tom grinned. "The sea's done the washing-up for us *and* put everything away!"

"But where?" Alex laughed.

Tom shrugged. "Now we'll *really* have to be like Robinson Crusoe."

The rest of their time on the island brought father and son closer and closer together. With the problems of simply surviving the next few days, they had to work as a team.

Together, they laid out everything in the sun to dry. Together, they sat on rocks and waited patiently for the fish to bite their hooks. And together, after they had spent an hour blowing on the damp paper and wood, they finally lit a fire. And all the time, they talked.

Finally, Alex felt confident enough to ask the question he had wanted to ask all along.

"Why did you leave me?" asked Alex.

"I left the *situation*," Tom said quietly. And he explained how he had always wanted to travel and how – although he was sorry to say it – his marriage to Alison had been a mistake. For them both.

"I just wasn't ready," he said. "And Alison gave up her studies. I still feel guilty about that. She was so intelligent. Like you," he added.

"So what did you do after you left home?" Alex asked.

"I travelled," he said simply. "South America, Africa, the Middle East, the Far East, China ... you name it, I've been there."

"You must have been so bored with us," Alex said sadly.

"Oh, Alex! I wasn't bored with you – either of you. And if Alison had come with me I'd have been the happiest man alive." He looked thoughtful. "It was the nice little house! The television and the washing-machine. The bills. The alarm clock. All those little things that remind you that you've become an adult. I didn't want to grow up that quickly. You understand, don't you?"

And, of course, Alex understood only too well.

That night, when Tom had gone to sleep, he picked up his diary and began writing.

Friday, 8 February

I've been in Australia for a month today. And it's been wonderful. If this is what "travel" is all about, then I want more! There is so much to see that the thought of settling in one place is awful.

I now know how trapped Tom must have felt all those years ago. I always thought he was wrong to leave us, but now I am not so sure. It would have been worse if he'd stayed, and been unhappy. Tom and Peter are so different from one another – how lucky I am to have them both!

Two more nights on Whitsunday Island! Since the rain stopped, it's been amazing. Sometimes I think I'd like to stay here for ever.

On the other hand, I really miss Dani!

Chapter eight

Up to the top ...

After the peace and quiet of Whitsunday Island, it came as a shock to be back on the mainland highway once more. As they drove back to Sydney, everything seemed so noisy, so crowded, so busy.

The second half of their desert island adventure had been perfect. There was no more rain. In fact, they didn't see a single cloud. By day, they swam, snorkelled, fished and lay in the hot sun; by night, they slept outside. It was warm and still, and the stars had never looked brighter. As if to remind Alex where he was, the brightest constellation was the Southern Cross which can only be seen south of the equator – and which decorates the Australian flag.

As he looked up at it on their last night, Alex noticed a shooting star sliding across the sky. He smiled.

"I wish I could travel for ever," he had whispered.

They arrived home late afternoon that Sunday.

"There you are!" Mary exclaimed as they walked into the kitchen. "We expected you back yesterday."

"But Tom always gets delayed," Alex laughed. "You should know that."

"Well, this time it could be serious," said Mary. "Dani's been trying to reach you all day. The band needs you to play at seven o'clock."

"Where?" asked Alex.

"Channel 9," said Mary.

"What, on television?" said Alex excitedly. "But, why?"

Mary smiled. "Dani'll explain everything." She looked at her watch. "You've got two hours, and the taxi will get you there in ten minutes. So you've got time for a shower. And this time I insist. You're filthy!"

Alex arrived at the Television Studios at half past five. He explained who he was to the man on the door, and was taken through to the dressing rooms.

"Alex!" Dani shouted. She ran towards him with her arms open, and closed them around him tightly. "I'm so glad you got here!" she said.

"So, what's all this about?" Alex asked.

"You mean you don't know?" said Dani, and looked at him in surprise.

"Haven't you been listening to the radio?" asked Terry.

Alex shook his head. "No," he said. "And I haven't watched any television, or read a newspaper either."

"Where have you *been*?" Dani asked.

Alex just laughed. "You tell me why we're here first," he said.

"We're on *The Chart Show*," Joe said.

"You mean we're in the top ten?" said Alex.

"Better than that," said Dani. "We're at number one!"

From then on, life for *The Beat Crew* became unbelievably hectic. As their single was selling so well nationally, their manager arranged a tour all over the country.

Alex's wish had come true! And how! It was as if his whole life had turned into a fairy-tale. And with no time to describe the events in detail, he simply wrote notes in his diary, to remind himself later, just how magical his life had become.

Sunday 11 February – concert Sydney. Monday 12 February – afternoon, radio interview; evening, concert Newcastle. Tuesday 13 February, – afternoon, film video; evening, concert Parramatta. Wednesday 14 February – morning, flight to Perth, "Jumpy" still at number one. Thursday 15 February – "Rhythms of the Beat Crew" in the shops! afternoon and evening, concerts in Perth. Saturday 16 February – morning, interview with music magazine; evening, concert in Fremantle ...

And so it went on. Non-stop bookings, one after the other after the other. Non-stop travel – first-class now, of course. And a non-stop succession of screaming crowds, expensive hotels and late-night parties.

What was more, everyone suddenly wanted to know about the "unknown" English bass guitarist of the country's newest pop sensation. He was interviewed by magazine and newspaper reporters. He appeared on the radio, on the television – in videos and on talk-shows. And wherever he went, Alex saw the new photo of the band, with himself grinning happily on posters, T-shirts, album covers and adverts.

Alex was on cloud nine!

"So, how do you like the limelight, then?" Dani asked

"Do you really need to ask?" Alex grinned. "I *love* it!"

Dani kissed him. "You're like a kid in a toyshop!" she said.

"That's just how I feel," Alex agreed.

The tour, which had taken them to every corner of Australia, had finally brought them to Byron Bay – the place they had almost visited all those months earlier. It was 18 April, and Alex and Dani were using the opportunity of a free afternoon to look round.

They were standing at the top of the lighthouse and looking down at the sea below them. It was as clear as glass.

"I love this place," said Dani. "I used to come here when I was a girl.

Alex thought of the other places he had seen. The Queensland rain forest, St Mary's Peak, ... Byron Bay was *nice*, but it didn't seem that special – and he said as much to Dani.

She smiled. "You just wait!" she said.

When Alex first saw the movement in the water, he thought it was another shark. But then, as the creature jumped up, bounced back on its tail and chattered loudly, he saw that it wasn't even a fish.

"A dolphin," he whispered excitedly, and grinned. They had always been his favourite animals.

"Not just one," said Dani. "Look!"

She was right. As if they had answered his call, ten ..., eleven ..., twelve more dolphins joined the first. Together, they swam round and round – they jumped, they dived, they chased each other's tails. They looked as if they were having fun. They looked as if they were playing.

And then, as suddenly as they had appeared, so they were gone again.

Dani sighed. "Just like us," she said. "Always on the move."

Alex looked at her, but said nothing. He had been thinking exactly the opposite.

He and Dani had grown close on the tour. They were now *a couple* and shared a room wherever they stayed. This did not mean, however, that they always agreed. Far from it. But these days, Alex seldom argued. He had learned that Dani usually had good reasons for the things she said.

But not this time! This time he was sure she was wrong.

The dolphins are not like us at all, he thought. *They* travel where they want, and there is no one to tell them where to go. *We* only travel to places where we are wanted. *They* will be able to continue as long as they like. *We* will have to stop if our songs don't sell enough.

They are free. *We* are not.

Chapter nine

... and down to earth

All good things come to an end – that's what people say. But did it have to happen so soon? Alex thought sadly. He'd never thought of himself as superstitious, yet later he wondered whether his thoughts at Byron Bay had had an influence on what followed. Perhaps it was because of the number of dolphins they had seen. Unlucky thirteen! Certainly, from then on things started to go wrong.

Violent storms that evening caused serious floods throughout the area, and when they finally came on stage, *The Beat Crew* found themselves in front of a half-empty hall. What was more, they had only played three songs when a power cut brought the concert to an early end. In some ways this was a good thing. Joe was so drunk that he had been hardly able to play his saxophone.

Joe and Pete had always drunk more than was good for them, but since their number one hit, they had both gone wild. Wine, women and song – and anything else they could think of. They had money in their pockets for the first time ever and were enjoying spending it. They would disappear into town for hours. And when they finally turned up – late for rehearsals – they would be too drunk to play properly.

"You only get one chance. Don't blow it!" Bob, their manager had warned them. "Success that comes quickly can disappear just as quickly."

But Joe and Pete hadn't listened. They were famous. They could do whatever they liked. While Dani and Alex had been watching the dolphins, Joe and Pete – drunk, as usual – had visited the local barber's and had their heads shaved.

"But why?" Terry demanded to know back at the hotel.

Joe grinned and took a mouthful of beer. "Fancied something cooler, didn't we?" he said.

"*The Beat Crew* is a fun group," said Alex. "Friendly ..."

"Boy-next-door," Dani added.

"Not a gang of skinheads," said Terry.

But neither of them were sorry for what they'd done.

"I don't want to look fun!" said Pete.

"Or friendly," Joe added menacingly. "I'm sick of being nice! I'm ... Oh, forget it! Come on, Pete, I'm going down to the bar."

And with that the pair of them stomped out of the room.

Over the next couple of weeks, it wasn't only problems *inside* the band which *The Beat Crew* had to deal with. For their next single, they decided to record a slow number called *Hugging Me*. Unfortunately, no one else agreed with this choice. Their video was never shown on television; the song was hardly ever played on the radio and, not surprisingly, the single didn't sell.

For the following single, they picked a bouncy number again. It was called *Sun Dance,* and came out at the beginning of June. By this time, however, no one seemed interested that *The Beat Crew* had returned to fast songs. As Bob said, "Yesterday's news is tomorrow's fish and chip paper!"

As the weeks passed, people forgot about *The Beat Crew*. The group became just one more in a long line of one-hit-wonders. The interviews stopped, the album stopped selling and their concerts were filled with people who fancied a dance, and didn't care what group was playing.

Terry, Alex and Dani tried to reverse the situation. They put all their energy into every performance, and tried hard to write a song that would do as well as *Jumpy*. But it was hopeless. Things were going from bad to worse, and all three of them knew that with Joe and Pete in the band, the band would never do well again.

If success had turned Joe and Pete wild, then lack of success had left them bitter and angry. They had started hanging round with a group of skinheads that Joe had known at school. The gang started coming to the band's gigs. They would start fights with people in the audience they didn't like the look of. And later, together with Joe and Pete, they would roam the streets, and look for trouble.

When Joe had *White Power* tattooed on his arm, even Pete knew he had gone too far. It was no longer a game.

The band finally hit rock bottom on Sunday, 24 June. They had been booked to play at the *Astoria* in the south-west suburbs of Sydney. From start to finish that day, nothing went right.

When they'd left, the van had refused to start. The new van had, by now, become as unreliable as the one it had replaced. And, although it didn't take long to repair it, no one cheered as *The Beat Crew* finally drove away. No one said a word. The day before they had asked Bob for a *new* van. It was only then that they discovered how little they had actually earned from their short period of success.

"All the parties, the promotion, the hotels – the money had to come from somewhere," Bob had explained.

They'd argued, of course, but when they looked at their contract a little more closely, they saw they had been legally cheated out of 90% of what they'd earned. And there was nothing they could do about it.

Now that their album and singles weren't selling, the parties and promotion had, of course, disappeared. And as for the hotels!

Alex looked around the dark, dirty room with its broken window and no hot water. He sighed. Four months earlier, he would have been happy. Just to be in a band had been enough then. But now that he had tasted the good life – room-service and silk sheets – it made the guesthouse all the more unpleasant.

"Come on," he said to Dani. "Let's get to the *Astoria*. It can't be worse than this."

But Alex was wrong. It *was* worse. Far worse.

The *Astoria* had been a cinema, and when it closed down the manager had simply taken away the seats and opened it up as a club. It had never been popular, and on the night *The Beat Crew* was going to play, fewer than a hundred people turned up.

But the band gave their best and, to begin with, everything went well enough. Then, however, during the fourth number, someone left of the stage threw a can of beer at Joe. It hit him on the side of the head. Beer and blood ran down onto his bomber jacket.

At first Alex thought that someone had objected to the mad-elephant noises his saxophone was making, but when the same part of the crowd began to shout "Racists out!", again and again, he realized it was not Joe's *music* they disliked.

To the Vietnamese and Greeks in the audience, Joe and Pete's presence was an insult. Now they had the opportunity to get their own back for the times they had been beaten up on the street. The beer can which hit Joe was just the first of many. Soon, the air was filled with flying metal and glass.

The situation was made worse by Joe and Pete's new-found friends. The moment Joe had been hit, they had jumped up to help him. A fight began. It was pandemonium. The band stopped playing, but the fight continued. The house lights went on, but *still* the fight continued. And it would have continued for a very long time if the police hadn't arrived.

With the situation under control at last, the band – minus Joe and Pete, who had disappeared when the police arrived – returned to their tiny dressing room. No one spoke.

"That was a disaster!" said Terry finally.

Dani and Alex looked at him. They could only agree.

Back at the guesthouse later that night, Dani lay on the bed. She was turning the pages of a magazine. Alex watched her. She was not reading, and he knew she was too upset to concentrate.

There was something that he wanted to talk to her about. Something important. But somehow, it never seemed like the right time. Certainly, here in the awful room, an hour after their disastrous gig, it was neither the time *nor* the place. Dani turned round and smiled.

Then she said, "You've got that *look* again. What's the matter?"

"Nothing," Alex lied.

"Things *will* get better again," she said. "You'll see."

Alex smiled. He didn't mind if she thought that it was the concert which was making him so quiet. The real reason could wait.

"When did Joe get that tattoo?" he asked. "What's the matter with him?" he said.

Dani shrugged. "He's always had a really mean streak in him," she said.

"We had so much," Alex said, sadly. "And now we're back where we started. Worse!" he said.

Dani nodded. "I'll never play with either of them again," she said. "And we'll have to change the name of the band," she added. "*The Beat Crew* will never get any bookings again. Not after tonight. But if we work at it ..."

"Work!" said Alex. "That's all we ever do."

"I always told you it was just a job," said Dani.

"Yeah," said Alex. "But you never said what a lousy job it could be."

Dani looked at him furiously. "It's a job that I love," she said. "That's why I struggled for two long, exhausting years. I *earned* my success. Not like you! And if you don't like the job, Alex, then you know what you can do. Resign!"

And with that she returned to her magazine. Alex stared at her back. He understood why she was so angry. Things had already been bad. Now they were beyond repair. In half an hour, everything she had worked for in the band had been destroyed.

Alex wanted to hug her. He wanted to say sorry. But how could he? If they hugged, they would talk. And if they talked, Alex would have to tell her the dilemma he was in. And if he did that, Dani herself would be destroyed.

That morning he had received two letters. In one of them was his passport. When the band had been doing well, Alex had applied to stay an extra six months. His extension had been granted. Now, Alex wished it hadn't. The other letter was from his mum and, although it was nice enough, the p.s. had troubled him.

I'm enclosing the book list which the university sent you. I know you're having a wonderful time, but don't forget your promise! Don't make the same mistake as me!!

Alex continued to look at Dani's back as conflicting thoughts filled his head. He *had* promised his mum that he'd take up his place at the university – that was all part of the deal. But he couldn't leave Dani; not now. And he still wanted to travel – not get stuck in one place. Then again, even Tom had settled down in the end. One day *he* would also have to, and what would he do without any qualifications?

Alex's head was spinning. Should he leave Austalia, or should he stay? Should he listen to his head or his heart? And who should he let down, Dani or his mum? They were impossible questions. Questions he *had* to talk over with someone else.

At that moment, a flake of paint fell from the ceiling and dropped down towards the bed. It landed on Dani's shoulder. She screamed.

"What is it? What is it?"

Alex gasped. "It's a cockroach," he said. "The biggest one I've ever seen!"

"GET IT OFF ME!!!" she shouted.

Alex moved towards the bed, leant over and flicked the

dried paint from Dani's shoulder. It landed on the floor and crumbled to dust. Dani looked at it for a second and turned round.

"You bastard!" she screamed.

Alex struggled in vain to keep a straight face. "I'm ... I'm sorry," he laughed.

"You're nothing but a stupid little kid!" Dani shouted.

A little kid, Alex thought. Like someone else I know!

He remembered the event with the shark; with the horse – and he knew that he had acted exactly the way Tom Connell would have done.

Like father, like son, he thought. And if that's so, then what would Tom Connell do in my situation now?

There was only one way to find out!

Chapter ten

New Year's Eve

Tuesday, 31 December

So it's the end of another year. I've just read through the whole diary – and what a year I've had! FANTASTIC! Kangaroo Island, surfing, the rain forest, Whitsunday Island, The Beat Crew. It's amazing how much you can pack in! If next year is half as good, I'll be happy.

Of course, it had its ups and downs, but when I look back, none of the bad bits were that bad! The worst day was 24 June. That disastrous concert in the old cinema! But even that had its positive side. After all, if the band hadn't broken up I wouldn't be here now.

I can still see the look on Tom's face when I talked to him about the decision I had to make. He was so shocked. "But this is history repeating itself," he said, as I went through the pros and cons of staying in Australia.

And then his advice ...

"You think you've got the choice between leaving Dani and going to university. Right? But it's not an either/or question, is it? There's a third possibility. You could combine the two!"

Thank you, Tom. If it hadn't been for you, I don't know what I'd be doing now. As it is, things couldn't have worked out better.

Bye bye, old year! Welcome to the new!

At that moment, the door opened and a head appeared.

"Are you coming down? Peter has got the champagne out."

Alex looked up. "Come here," he said. "I've got something to tell you."

Dani walked over to the bed and lay down next to him. "What is it?" she asked.

"You don't regret coming to England, do you?" he asked.

"Regret it?" she said. "Of course not."

"Sure?"

"For a start, if I hadn't come here, I wouldn't be doing my music degree. Secondly, I wouldn't be in Britain's newest up-and-coming pop sensation."

Alex smiled. To earn a bit of extra money the pair of them played in local pubs three nights a week. They called themselves *The Dolphins*, and were gaining quite a reputation. Two nights earlier, someone from a record company had approached them. This time, however, they were careful. They took the man's card and promised to contact him. Certainly, they were not going to sign *anything* until they'd read the small print very carefully.

"And third," Dani continued, "I wouldn't be with you! No, for me things couldn't have worked out better."

Alex smiled. "That's just what I wrote in my diary," he said.

"Was that all you wanted to say?" said Dani, as she sat up. "We really should ..."

"No," Alex interrupted. "I wanted to tell you this. I love you, Danielle Louise Klavans," he said.

Dani smiled as she leant down to kiss him. "And do you know what, Alexander Patrick Connell? I love you too."

Alex pulled away. He had decided not to change his name in the end. It had been wonderful meeting Tom at last but, because of the years they hadn't spent together, Alex felt they could never be more than friends. Certainly they were similar in many ways, but it was Peter Reid who had brought him up, not Tom. Peter was the one he had called "dad" all his life.

Before the trip, he had thought it would be ungrateful to change his name. Now that the trip was over, there was something else. Alex knew he could never isolate himself from the family he loved so much.

"It's Alexander Patrick *Reid*," he said quietly.

"Whatever," Dani said, and smiled. "Come on. It's five to midnight. Let's go downstairs and wish the rest of the Reid family a Happy New Year."

Vocabulary

pl. = plural, *n.* = noun, *sb.* = somebody, *sth.* = something

A (to) **abandon** [ə'bændn] verlassen
Aboriginal [æbə'rɪdʒənl] eingeboren; australische/r Ureinwohner/in
about: What is it all about? Worum handelt es sich eigentlich?
(to) **advertise sth.** ['ædvətaɪz] für etwas Werbung machen
after all schließlich
alarm clock [ə'lɑːm klɒk] Wecker
album ['ælbəm] Album *(LP oder CD)*
amazing [ə'meɪzɪŋ] erstaunlich
amphitheatre ['æmfɪθɪətə] Amphitheater
anchor ['æŋkə] Anker
appearance on television [ə'pɪərəns] Fernsehauftritt
applause [ə'plɔːz] Applaus, Beifall
(to) **approach sb.** [ə'prəʊtʃ] sich jm. nähern, auf jn. zukommen
audience ['ɔːdɪəns] Publikum, Anhänger(schaft)
(to) **audition** [ɔː'dɪʃn] vorspielen
Aussie ['ɒzɪ] *(umgangssprachlich für)* australisch; Australier/in
awkward ['ɔːkwəd] unbeholfen

B **backpack** ['bækpæk] Rucksack
backstage drink [bæk'steɪdʒ] Drink hinter der Bühne/in der Garderobe
(to) **bang** [bæŋ] knallen
barber ['bɑːbə] (Herren-)Friseur
barrier ['bærɪə] Schranke
basker ['bɑːskə] *harmlose Haiart*

bass guitarist [beɪs gɪ'tɑ:rɪst] Baßgitarrist/in
bastard ['bɑ:stəd] gemeiner Kerl
beer [bɪə] Bier
bent: (to) **bend down, bent, bent** [bend, bent, bent] sich nach vorn beugen
better: you'd better do ... du solltest lieber ... tun
(to) **bite the hook** [baɪt, hʊk] anbeißen *(Fische)*
bleach [bli:tʃ] Bleichmittel
blood [blʌd] Blut
(to) **blow sth.** [bləʊ] etwas vermasseln
(to) **blush** [blʌʃ] erröten, rot werden
(to) **body surf** ['bɒdɪ sɜ:f] surfen
booking ['bʊkɪŋ] *hier:* Termin
bottled-up feelings ['bɒtld] aufgestaute Gefühle
(to) **bounce back** [baʊns] zurückprallen
bouncy ['baʊnsɪ] federnd, elastisch
boy-next-door *etwa:* wie der guterzogene Jungen von nebenan
(to) **break away from** (sich) losbrechen von
breaker ['breɪkə] Brecher, Sturzwelle
breakdown truck ['breɪkdaʊn trʌk] Abschleppwagen
breath [breθ] Atem
(to) **bring up children** Kinder großziehen
butterfly ['bʌtəflaɪ] Schmetterling

C **calf** [kɑ:f] Kalb
casino [kə'si:nəʊ] Spielkasino
(to) **catch the sun** ein bißchen zuviel Sonne abbekommen
cement [sə'ment] Zement
champagne [ʃæm'peɪn] Champagner, Sekt
Channel 9 ['tʃænl] Kanal 9
(to) **chase** [tʃeɪs] Jagd machen auf
(to) **chatter** ['tʃætə] schnattern

(to) **cheat sb. out of sth.** [tʃi:t] jn. um etwas betrügen
cheek [tʃi:k] Wange, Backe
(to) **cheer up** [tʃɪə] wieder fröhlich werden
cheerful(ly) ['tʃɪəfəl(ɪ)] fröhlich, vergnügt
cherry ['tʃerɪ] Kirsche
(to) **clap** [klæp] Beifall klatschen, applaudieren
(to) **clean off** [kli:n] abputzen
cleaner ['kli:nə] Reinigungsmittel
client ['klaɪənt] Klient/in, Kunde/Kundin
(to) **cling to** [klɪŋ] festhalten
(to) **close down** [kləʊz] *(ein Geschäft)* schließen
cloud: (to) be on cloud nine im siebten Himmel schweben
cockroach ['kɒkrəʊtʃ] (Küchen-)Schabe
(to) **concentrate on** ['kɒnsəntreɪt] sich konzentrieren auf
concerned: as far as I'm concerned [kən'sɜ:nd] was mich betrifft
conflicting [kən'flɪktɪŋ] widersprüchlich
constellation [kɒnstə'leɪʃn] Sternbild
contract ['kɒntrækt] Vertrag
cool [ku:l] kühl
coral ['kɒrl] Korallenstock
countless ['kaʊntləs] zahllos
crater ['kreɪtə] Krater
creature ['kri:tʃə] Geschöpf, Tier
crew [kru:] Mannschaft
criticism ['krɪtɪsɪzm] Vorwurf
(to) **criticize** ['krɪtɪsaɪz] kritisieren
crocodile ['krɒkədaɪl] Krokodil
crook [krʊk] Betrüger/in
cross: Southern Cross [krɒs] Kreuz des Südens
(to) **crumble** ['krʌmbl] zerfallen
cry [kraɪ] Schrei
cupped hand [kʌpt] gewölbte Hand

current ['kʌrənt] Strömung
customs ['kʌstəmz] Zoll

D **damp** [dæmp] feucht
(to) **dart** [dɑːt] sich blitzschnell bewegen
decisive(ly) [dɪ'saɪsɪv(lɪ)] entschieden, entschlossen
defensive [dɪ'fensɪv] verteidigend, schützend
(to) **delay** [dɪ'leɪ] aufhalten
delight [dɪ'laɪt] Entzücken
dense [dens] dicht
dent [dent] Beule, Delle
description [dɪ'skrɪpʃn] Beschreibung
(to) **disappear** [dɪsə'pɪə] verschwinden
disagreement [dɪsə'griːmənt] Meinungsverschiedenheit
disaster [dɪ'zɑːstə] Katastrophe
disastrous [dɪ'zɑːstrəs] katastrophal, verheerend
disinfectant [dɪsɪn'fektənt] Desinfektionsmittel
(to) **disturb** [dɪ'stɜːb] stören
dolphin ['dɒlfɪn] Delphin
downpour ['daʊnpɔː] Platzregen
drawing ['drɔːɪŋ] Zeichnung
drip, drip, drip [drɪp] Tröpfeln
drizzle ['drɪzl] Nieselregen
drum [drʌm] Trommel
drummer ['drʌmə] Trommler/in
due: (to) **be due to** [djuː] etwas tun müssen *oder* sollen
dune [djuːn] Düne

E **embarrassed** [ɪm'bærəst] verlegen
emu ['iːmjuː] Emu *(straußenähnlicher Laufvogel)*
energy ['enədʒɪ] Energie, Kraft

(to) **enclose** [ɪn'kləʊz] beifügen
(to) **entertain** [entə'teɪn] unterhalten
equator [ɪ'kweɪtə] Äquator
(to) **exclaim** [ɪk'skleɪm] (aus)rufen
exhausting [ɪg'zɔːstɪŋ] anstrengend, strapaziös
(to) **exist** [ɪg'zɪst] existieren
exotic [ɪg'zɒtɪk] exotisch, fremdartig
(to) **explode** [ɪk'spləʊd] explodieren
(to) **extend** [ɪk'stend] verlängern
extension: his extension had been granted [ɪk'stenʃn, grɑːntɪd] sein Antrag auf Verlängerung war bewilligt worden
eyebrow ['aɪbraʊ] Augenbraue

F (to) **fail** [feɪl] *hier:* ausbleiben
fairy-tale ['feərɪteɪl] Märchen
familiar [fə'mɪlɪə] vertraut, bekannt
(to) **fancy** ['fænsɪ] Lust haben auf
fatherless ['fɑːðələs] vaterlos
fear [fɪə] Furcht, Angst
fearless ['fɪələs] furchtlos
filthy ['fɪlθɪ] schmutzig, dreckig
fin [fɪn] Flosse
(to) **flag sb. down** [flæg] jn. anhalten
flake [fleɪk] Flocke
(to) **flash** [flæʃ] sich blitzartig bewegen, rasen
(to) **flick** [flɪk] schnippen
flipper ['flɪpə] (Schwimm-)Flosse
fly, *pl.:* **flies** [flaɪ(z)] Fliege
(to) **fold up** [fəʊld] zusammenfalten
for ever [fər‿'evə] für immer
(to) **forgive** [fə'gɪv] verzeihen, vergeben
four-wheel drive [fɔːwiːl 'draɪv] (Auto mit) Allradantrieb

frantical(ly) ['fræntɪkl(ɪ)] *hier:* hektisch
furious(ly) ['fjʊərɪəs(lɪ)] wütend, zornig

G (to) **gasp** [gɑːsp] nach Luft schnappen
(to) **get lost** [lɒst] sich verirren
(to) **get to know** (sich) kennenlernen
gig [gɪg] Auftritt
(to) **go ahead: You go ahead.** Nur zu! Mach nur!
good-looking [gʊd'lʊkɪŋ] gutaussehend
(to) **grab** [græb] hastig packen, schnappen
(to) **grate** [greɪt] knirschen
(to) **grin** [grɪn] grinsen; verschmitzt lächeln
(to) **groan** [grəʊn] (auf)stöhnen
guilty ['gɪltɪ] schuldig
gypsy ['dʒɪpsɪ] Zigeuner/in

H **halt** [hɔːlt] Halt
handle ['hændl] Klinke, Griff
(to) **have a sleep** ein Schläfchen machen
(to) **hesitate** ['hezɪteɪt] zögern
highway ['haɪweɪ] Haupt(verkehrs)straße
hypnotic [hɪp'nɒtɪk] hypnotisierend

I **idiot** ['ɪdɪət] Idiot/in
impressed [ɪm'prest] beeindruckt
indeed [ɪn'diːd] in der Tat, tatsächlich
insignificant [ɪnsɪg'nɪfɪkənt] unbedeutend, unwichtig
(to) **insist** [ɪn'sɪst] bestehen (auf)
insult ['ɪnsult] Beleidigung
(to) **interrupt** [ɪntə'rʌpt] unterbrechen
irritation [ɪrɪ'teɪʃn] Verärgerung, Ärger
(to) **isolate oneself from** ['aɪsəleɪt] sich trennen von

J **jack** [dʒæk] Wagenheber
jumpy ['dʒʌmpɪ] nervös

K (to) **kick** [kɪk] stoßen, treten
koala [kəʊ'ɑːlə] Koalabär

L (to) **label** ['leɪbl] etikettieren
lack of [læk] Mangel an
lagoon [lə'guːn] Lagune *(durch einen Landstreifen vom offenen Meer getrennter flacher Meeresteil)*
laid: (to) **lay, laid, laid** [leɪ, leɪd, leɪd] legen
lay down: (to) **lie down, lay, lain** [laɪ, leɪ, leɪn] sich hinlegen
leant down: (to) **lean down, leant, leant** [liːn, lent, lent] sich verbeugen
liana [lɪ'ɑːnə] Liane, Kletterpflanze
lifetime ['laɪftaɪm] Leben(szeit)
lighthouse ['laɪthaʊs] Leuchtturm
limelight ['laɪmlaɪt] Rampenlicht
line [laɪn] Reihe
lit: (to) **light, lit, lit** [lait, lɪt, lɪt] anzünden
(to) **look fun** *etwa:* lässig aussehen
loose [luːs] lose
lounge [laʊndʒ] Wartehalle
lousy ['laʊzɪ] mies
Ltd. = Limited [lɪmɪtɪd] GmbH (Gesellschaft mit beschränkter Haftung)

M **macho** ['mætʃəʊ] (betont) männlich
magical ['mædʒɪkl] märchenhaft
mainland ['meɪnlənd] Festland

mainland USA ['meɪnlənd] USA ohne Alaska und Hawaii
mangrove swamp ['mæŋgrəʊv 'swɒmp] Mangrovensumpf
(to) **make it up to sb.** etwas wiedergutmachen
marriage ['mærɪdʒ] Ehe
mate [meɪt] Kumpel
menacing(ly) ['menəsɪŋ(lɪ)] drohend
mess [mes] Durcheinander
mind: in mind [maɪnd] *hier:* im Hinterkopf
miserable ['mɪzərəbl] unglücklich
mist [mɪst] Nebel
modest(ly) ['mɒdɪst(lɪ)] bescheiden
(to) **moor** [mʊə] festgemacht/vertäut liegen
mountainside ['maʊntɪnsaɪd] Berg(ab)hang
muddy ['mʌdɪ] schlammig
(to) **mutter** ['mʌtə] murmeln

N **neither did the next car** auch das nächste Auto nicht
nightmare ['naɪtmeə] Alptraum
none [nʌn] keine(r, s)
note [nəʊt] Note
now and then von Zeit zu Zeit
nuisance: (to) **be a nuisance** ['nju:səns] lästig fallen, nerven

O (to) **object to** [əb'dʒekt] etwas gegen eine Sache (einzuwenden) haben
off: I've got some time off [ɒf] ich habe ein paar Tage Urlaub/ein paar Tage frei
oncoming ['ɒnkʌmɪŋ] entgegenkommend
on the other hand andererseits

optimistic [ɒptɪ'mɪstɪk] optimistisch
Outback ['aʊtbæk] Busch, Hinterland (Australiens)

P **palm tree** [pɑːm] Palme
pandemonium [pændə'məʊnɪ͜əm] Hölle
paradise ['pærədaɪs] Paradies
Pardon? ['pɑːdən] Wie bitte?
passage ['pæsɪdʒ] *hier:* Kanal
passport ['pɑːspɔːt] Paß
peak [piːk] (Berg-)Spitze
performance [pə'fɔːməns] Vorstellung
photocopy ['fəʊtəʊkɒpɪ] Fotokopie
plaintive ['pleɪntɪv] klagend
pom [pɒm] *umgangssprachliche Bezeichnung für britische Einwanderin/britischen Einwanderer (in Australien oder Neuseeland)*
positive ['pɒzətɪv] positiv
possum ['pɒsəm] Opossum
pot [pɒt] Topf
power cut ['paʊə kʌt] Stromausfall
(to) **pray** [preɪ] beten
presence ['prezəns] Gegenwart
(to) **pretend** [prɪ'tend] so tun als ob
promotion [prə'məʊʃn] Förderung, Begünstigung
(to) **prove** [pruːv] beweisen
(to) **pull away** sich freimachen
(to) **pull oneself together** sich zusammenreißen, -nehmen
pump [pʌmp] Pumpe
(to) **put up with** ruhig hinnehmen

Q **quiet** ['kwaɪət] Ruhe, Stille

R **racist** ['reɪsɪst] Rassist/in
(to) **raise** [reɪz] hochziehen
rear-window ['rɪə'wɪndəʊ] Heckscheibe
reception [rɪ'sepʃn] (Hotel-)Rezeption
(to) **reconnect** [ri:kə'nekt] wieder anschließen, verbinden
reef [ri:f] Riff
regret [rɪ'gret] Reue, Bedauern
(to) **regret** [rɪ'gret] bedauern, bereuen
rehearsal [rɪ'hɜ:sl] Probe
remote [rɪ'məʊt] abgelegen
(to) **replace** [rɪ'pleɪs] ersetzen
reputation [repjʊ'teɪʃn] Ruf
(to) **rescue** ['reskju:] retten
reserve [rɪ'zɜ:v] Reservat, Schutzgebiet
(to) **resign** [rɪ'zaɪn] *hier:* aufhören
reunion [ri:'ju:nɪ͜ən] Wiedersehen, Zusammenkunft
(to) **reunite** [ri:jʊ'naɪt] sich wieder verein(ig)en
(to) **reverse sth.** [rɪ'vɜ:s] etwas umkehren
rhythm ['rɪðm] Rhythmus
rice [raɪs] Reis
ridiculous [rɪ'dɪkjʊləs] lächerlich
rip [rɪp] Strömung
(to) **roam** [rəʊm] durchstreifen
rock bottom [rɒk 'bɒtm] Tiefpunkt

S **sarcastic(ally)** [sɑ:'kæstɪk(lɪ)] sarkastisch
saxophone ['sæksəfəʊn] Saxophon
(to) **scream** [skri:m] schreien
(to) **screech** [skri:tʃ] *hier:* quietschen
sea anemone ['si: ə'nemənɪ] Seeanemone
seal [si:l] Robbe
(to) **search** [sɜ:tʃ] suchen
secret *(n.)* ['si:krət] Geheimnis

seldom ['seldəm] selten
(to) **sell (well)** [sel] sich (gut) verkaufen
sense of humour ['sens‿əv 'hju:mə] Sinn für Humor
(to) **serve: It serves us right for lying to the police!** [sɜ:vz, laɪɪŋ] Das geschieht uns recht, wo wir die Polizei belogen haben!
set [set] *hier:* Serie, Folge
shadow [ʃædəʊ] Schatten
(to) **shake** [ʃeɪk] schütteln
shallow stream ['ʃæləʊ] seichtes Flüßchen
(to) **shave** [ʃeɪv] rasieren
(to) **shiver** ['ʃɪvə] frösteln, zittern
shoal of fish [ʃəʊl] Schwarm Fische
shooting star [ʃu:tɪŋ 'stɑ:] Sternschnuppe
(to) **shrug** [ʃrʌg] die Achseln zucken
(to) **sigh** [saɪ] seufzen
(to) **sign** [saɪn] unterschreiben
silk [sɪlk] Seide
(to) **slam** [slæm] zuknallen, zuschlagen
sleepily ['sli:pɪlɪ] schläfrig
(to) **slide** [slaɪd] gleiten
the small print [prɪnt] das Kleingedruckte
(to) **snorkel** ['snɔ:kl] schnorcheln
soaked [səʊkt] durchnäßt
soft(ly) [sɒft(lɪ)] sanft, leise
so much the better um so besser
sorrow ['sɒrəʊ] Kummer
spare room [speə] Gästezimmer
spare tyre [speə] Ersatzreifen
spinning: his head was spinning ['spɪnɪŋ] ihm schwirrte der Kopf
(to) **splash** [splæʃ] plantschen
spot [spɒt] (Farb-)Fleck
spotlight ['spɒtlaɪt] Rampenlicht
stage [steɪdʒ] Bühne

(I'm) starving ['stɑːvɪŋ] ich komme um vor Hunger
(to) **steam** [stiːm] dampfen
(to) **steer** [stɪə] steuern, lenken
stiff [stɪf] steif, starr
(to) **sting** [stɪŋ] stechen
(to) **stomp** [stɒmp] stampfen
straight: (to) **keep a straight face** [streɪt] das Gesicht nicht verziehen
streak: he's always had a really mean streak in him [striːk] er hat schon immer so einen gemeinen Zug an sich gehabt
(to) **stroke** [strəʊk] streicheln
struck: which struck Alex [strʌk] was Alex auffiel
stuck: (to) **be stuck** [stʌk] steckenbleiben, festsitzen
studies ['stʌdɪz] Studium
(to) **stumble** ['stʌmbl] stolpern
succession [sək'seʃn] (Aufeinander-)Folge
sugar cane ['ʃʊgə keɪn] Zuckerrohr
(to) **sulk** [sʌlk] schmollen, eingeschnappt sein
sulkily ['sʌlkɪ(lɪ)] schmollend
sunken ['sʌŋkn] versunken
sunstroke ['sʌnstrəʊk] Sonnenstich
suntan ['sʌntæn] (Sonnen-)Bräune
surface ['sɜːfɪs] Oberfläche
(to) **swallow** ['swɒləʊ] schlucken
sweaty ['swetɪ] verschwitzt, schweißnaß

T **tail** [teɪl] Schwanz
tarmac road ['tɑːmæk] Art geteerte Straße
taste of fame [teɪst, feɪm] Vorgeschmack von Ruhm
tattoo [tæ'tuː] Tätowierung
(to) **tattoo** [tæ'tuː] tätowieren
Thank heavens. ['hevnz] Gott sei Dank!
thud [θʌd] dumpfer Schlag

tide [taɪd] Flut
tiller ['tɪlə] Ruderpinne
toddler ['tɒdlə] Kleinkind
torrential rain(s) [tə'renʃl] sintflutartige Regenfälle
track [træk] Wanderweg
trainers ['treɪnəz] Trainingsschuhe
(to) **trap** [træp] (in einer Falle) fangen
triangle ['traɪæŋgl] Dreieck
trunks *(pl.)* [trʌŋks] Badehose
(to) **trust** [trʌst] (ver)trauen, glauben
(to) **turn on sb.** sich wenden gegen jdn.
turn-off ['tɜːnɒf] Abzweig(ung)

U **unbearable** [ʌn'beərəbl] unerträglich
(to) **undo** [ʌn'duː] ungeschehen machen
ungrateful [ʌn'greɪtfl] undankbar
unguarded [ʌn'gɑːdɪd] unbewacht
unreliable [ʌnrɪ'laɪəbl] unzuverlässig
up to bis
up-and-coming pop sensation [ʌpənkʌmɪŋ 'pɒp senseɪʃn] aufstrebende Popsensation
ups and downs Höhen und Tiefen
utensil [juː'tensl] Gerät

V **vague(ly)** [veɪg(lɪ)] vage
vain: in vain [veɪn] vergeblich
vastness ['vɑːstnəs] ungeheuere Größe
Victorian [vɪk'tɔːrɪən] viktorianisch

W (to) **waddle** ['wɒdl] watscheln
(to) **wade** [weɪd] waten
wanderer ['wɒndərə] Wanderer, Wanderin

wasp [wɒsp] Wespe
water-chute ['wɒtə ʃuːt] Wasserrutschbahn
What's all this about? Was ist hier eigentlich los?
while *(n.)* [waɪl] Weile
(to) **whisper** ['wɪspə] flüstern
Whitsunday [wɪt'sʌndɪ] Pfingstsonntag
(to) **wince** [wɪns] zusammenzucken
windscreen ['wɪndskriːn] Windschutzscheibe
winetasting ['waɪnteɪstɪŋ] Weinprobe
(to) **wink at sb.** [wɪnk] jm. zuzwinkern
(to) **work out: things couldn't have worked out better** die Dinge hätten nicht besser laufen können

Y **yacht** [jɒt] Yacht

Names

People's names

Alex/Alexander Patrick Reid ['æleks, ælɪg'zɑːndə pætrɪk 'riːd]
Alison Reid ['ælɪsn 'riːd]
Dani/Danielle Louise Klavans ['dænɪ, dænɪ'el lu'iːz 'klævns]
Danny ['dænɪ]
Dominic ['dɒmɪnɪk]
Kevin Williams ['wɪljəms]
Lucy ['luːsɪ]
Luke [luːk]
Ron [rɒn]
Tom Connell ['kɒnl]

Place names

Adelaide ['ædəleɪd]
Athens ['æθɪnz]
Barossa Valley [bə'rɒsə]

Bateman's Bay ['beɪtmənz]
Bondi Beach ['bɒndaɪ]
Brisbane ['brɪzbən]
Byron Bay ['baɪrən]
Cairns [keənz]
Coogee Bay ['kuːdʒiː]
Flinders Ranges ['flɪndəz reɪndʒɪz]
Fremantle ['friːmæntl]
Grafton Passage ['grɑːftn]
Great Barrier Reef [greɪt 'bærɪə riːf]
Hedley ['hedlɪ]
Mackay [mə'kaɪ]
Meadcross Road ['miːdkrɒs]
Melbourne ['melbən]
Newcastle ['njuːkɑːsl]
Parramatta [pærə'mætə]
Perth [pɜːθ]
Phillip Island ['fɪlɪp]
Pitcairn Avenue ['pɪtkeən]
Queensland ['kwiːnzlənd]
Rockhampton [rɒk'hæmtən]
Singapore [sɪŋə'pɔː]
Sydney ['sɪdnɪ]
Townsville ['taʊnzvɪl]
Whitsunday Island [wɪt'sʌndɪ]
Wilpena Pound [wɪl'piːnə 'paʊnd]

Other names
Angelo's ['ændʒələʊz]
Astoria [ə'stɔːrɪə]
Eudyptula minor [juː'dɪptjʊlə 'maɪnə]
KayCee ['keɪsiː]
Robinson Crusoe [rɒbɪnsn 'kruːsəʊ]
Sabrina's [sə'briːnəz]
Thekla ['θeklə]